Short History
of the Fur Trade

By *Adrien Stoutenburg*

Heroes, Advise Us
Short History of the Fur Trade

Short History
of the Fur Trade

Adrien Stoutenburg

Houghton Mifflin Company
Boston 1969

Portions of the title poem have appeared in The New Yorker under
the title "Trapper's Report" (Copyright © 1968, The New Yorker
Magazine, Inc.) and in Prairie Schooner under the title "Short
History of the Fur Trade" (Copyright © 1968, Prairie Schooner,
the University of Nebraska Press).

Other poems included here are reprinted by permission of the peri-
odicals where they first appeared: From Epoch, "Alchemist's Note-
book, Revised" and "Snob" (1966), "Specialists" (1967), and "Pil-
grimage" (1968). Epos, "Notice of Change of Residence" (1967).
Kayak, "Down, Under, Above," "Grade AA, Large," "Note to the
Outside," "California, Here I am" (1965), "Justice," "Night Call"
(1966), "Séance," "Telegram" (1967). Poetry Northwest, "Three
Predecessors" (1965), "Forms of Travel" and "Who Loves to Lie
With Me" (1967), "Science Non-Fiction"—now "Journey to the
Interior."—(1968). Red Clay Reader, "Snapshot" and "Flight" (1966).
Shenandoah, "Refugee" (1965) and "Private Beach" (1967).

The following poems appeared originally in The New Yorker:
"Avalanche" (1964), "Tree Service" (1966), "On the Wagon" and
"Subdivider" (1968).

Included in the Best Poems, Borestone Mountain Poetry Awards
series, were "Three Predecessors" (1965), "Tree Service" (1966),
"Who Loves to Lie With Me" and "Specialists" (1967).

Contents

Short History
of the Fur Trade

Short History
of the Fur Trade

Costume Book (Excerpt One)

Lions were always high style,
the tail, a bearded rope,
glowing from angular pharaohs' belts;
the paws, chrysanthemums with thorns,
flung over priestly torsos
in a dead embrace.
Nero used the whole beast beneath his throne,
its mane spread out like a yellow ocean's wave,
head hollowed, scooped, and stuffed,
the fangs intent as jewels,
the eyes (the footstool's staring radiance)
trapped under sandals beating time
to a tin lyre and the gusty cries
from torches shaped like burning rows of men.

Queen Semiramis, heiress of Babylon,
was fond of tigers, marched to India
with a million spears, reeled back before the roar
of elephants that rose like wrinkled walls,
but carried home a thousand skins
whose brown and supple lightning bolts
hummed like doves beneath her lingering hand.

Leopards, too, were popular
with those who could afford such flowers
blossoming on wall or couch,
as when the Great Khan, hunting
with his barons, cooks, and hawks,
set up his pointed cities on the trail,
covering each sable-curtained tent
with gardens stitched from golden hides
on which the dark geranium leaves
rippled in wind as if alive.

The fox's brush was popular with kings,
flared on the tips of lances
like a bushy flame, while Chinese mandarins
and Vandal lords yawned into bed
beneath the silk-lined plush
of weasel, moleskin, any soft, denuded thing
the hunters peeled and left
to stare at heaven through its sudden skull.

The poor made do with common pelts—
rabbit and dog, the soft brocade of cats—
but dreamed beneath their calluses and lice
of a new world where ermine flowed
to every poacher's trap,
seeing around them (a brittle fleece
scattered on alp and steppe and moor)
only the comfortless, dead white
of drift on drift of deepening bones.

Monarchs, too, felt the swift cold,
began to keep the rarer beasts
(thought-furrowed apes, gazelles, and deer)
in fountain-plumed menageries;
sent huntsmen sniffing toward fresh seas,
found beaver hats and otter muffs,
brown, booming robes of buffalo,
the neat pronghorn, the narrow wolf,
and grizzlies rearing up like shaggy towers—
      and then again
   the drift on drift of bones.

      The zoo preserves some specimens,
      the penny-colored lion, the shopworn
            bear,
      and tigers lend a spark to circuses,
      while delicate foxes with trade names
      (Royal Pastel, Starlight, and Silver
            Blue)
      pant through a fur farm's lethal door
      toward breathless evenings on Nob
            Hill,
      and Easter morning on Park Avenue.

O *Paradiso*

Cartier, hunting for China, found
   the polar bear, "big as a cow and white as a
      swan,"

and wapiti with antlers like stiff ferns;
    plunged into Canada, observed the smaller tribes
of animals, replacements for the vanished plush
    of a spent world, and copper-colored chiefs
wrapped carelessly in the deep silk
    of badger, marten, vixen, and mink,
while Tudor monarchs straddling tired thrones
    invaded monastaries, pawed at creaking shelves
for copes and chasubles outlined with fur.
    French nobles grieved to see
their sable-lined nightgowns grow thin—
    took heart when Cartier's first cargo came
gleaming to port; sent out fresh hunters:
    the beaver-eyed Champlain, and *coureurs de bois*
to rampage in primeval woods
    where thirsty Hurons, munching birds,
delivered raw, red kingdoms in exchange
    for fire sloshing in a drunken cup.
The Dutch sent Hudson sailing to an inland bay
    whose roadless shores shook with the gloss
and weight of beasts, enough to clothe a continent
    of dukes, freebooters, merchants, priests:
and, rounding all, awash with broken flowers,
    the fertile, green, and whale-backed sea.

John Jacob Astor

From the Black Forest where wooden birds
tethered in clocks outchimed the owl,
and the inverted pendulums of pine
ticked in the wind,
                    the butcher's son—
neck short as a stump, eyes quick as gold—
thumped in his boots up a Roman road
inlaid with the gristle of hart and hind
and the ghosts of kings: Charlemagne
tucked in an otter pelisse,
Attila (the Scourge of God) in bear,
Crusaders in fox, and ladies hunting,
folly bells sewn to cuff and tippet,
the silent dormouse scalloped with noise,
flesh turned to a boisterous silver . . .
                    the butcher's son tromping
toward the Rhine and the Lowlands,
unfurred, unschooled, his bundle swinging
like a cloth heart in the red springtime.

From the forest and Bristol toward Baltimore,
the steerage dark, the waves uneven,
the snow aslant, like the lip of a shark,
the Atlantic combed but snarled and snarling,
John Jacob retched in a wooden bunk
(his seven flutes hidden, fruit of his savings),
five guineas trapped in his crooning purse

7

(fingered and fondled, music of money),
stared toward the new world—heard overhead
the hot, furred step of executives
in charge of Indians, trinkets, toys,
and the beaver slapping his tail on water.

On a storm-white deck in a clotted sea,
the sweating regents of Hudson's Bay
(up to their jaws in windy pelts)
walked above the stiffening waves,
talking of weather and traps and trade
to the bobbing, bowing emigrant.
  Deft as a ferret, though thick in the waist,
  with a mallet jaw, and naked ears,
  listener, seeker, he caught a glimpse
  of towering gold.
                The ocean gleamed;
waves turned to castles, reflecting light
whirled up from the shores of another Eden
unguarded by angels, the wilderness spangled
with hoof, claw, feather, all for the taking,
forests laced and furrowed with trails
of hunters in buckskin bringing guns and whiskey
to wigwam and hogan.
                No capital needed,
for the ignorant savage, palms rank with ermine,
was blind with desire for ribbons and tinsel.

8

John Jacob, Junior, twenty-one,
with a twitch for profit, a tooth for gold,
tucked fact and dream in a miser's corner—
how to garner in winter, furbish and fold

the little garments of fox and weasel,
the capes of badgers, tunics of bear;
use of the fleshing knife and scraper,
the proper employment of trigger and snare

(avoidance of poison, which bleaches out
fur's natural russet, ripple, and sheen,
or bullets that batter more than the skull);
compared the pelage of wolverine

to the beaver's soft and guarded felt
in fashion with hatters everywhere,
prime pelts to swaddle the frigid ears
of Smith and Powhatan, Pepys and Voltaire,

Puritan and caliph, Tartar and Pope,
all blessed by the genus *castor*
aching in voyageurs' nimble traps
and the mind of John Jacob Astor.

Trapper's Report

They are domestic, faithful to their families,
   often work by moonlight,

clerks and engineers in brisk overcoats,
wearing keen incisors between wind-puffed
    cheeks,
comedians of poplars and ponds,
lovers of calculus
and the long blue sums of water,
subject, by nature, to seasons
of lightning and frost
but pitching always above muddy foundations
their precise households
with porches as round
as the white hearts of birches.

They are captured easily in winter
    in their domed cities.
When the light comes in with the hunter's axe,
and the bedroom floor—draped for darkness—
dazzles and blinks,
they run on their shoeless feet
to the sudden window,
confused by so early an April
and by the steep noose slung
around a low throat.

Hauled into day
    (out of the dusky, two-story chamber
    mattressed with summer and sleep,
    clean as dead wheat,

and mumbling with babies),
their whiskers sweat,
beaded like a red abacus.
  They are full of blood
  when slit down the belly
  from neck to crotch
  and also on the inside of each leg
  to the center cut,
      the outer garment then peeled off
      both ways toward the spine
      and stretched on an oval frame,
      the guard hairs plucked
      to leave, brown-rayed and warm,
      a breathless velvet hung
      against the white and ever-naked wind.

John Jacob Astor

Hawker, flute trader, entrepreneur
jostling pigs for the right of way
through Broadway mud, where the newly free
peddled tin copies of liberty bells
or dragged their independent carts
to mansions of a later royalty
(landlord, mayor, merchant, judge),
he dodged the ruts of common dreams—
and the uncommon hope of brotherhood—
concluding that equality

came easiest to those with bank accounts.
All else was sentiment,
a scroll tossed by the Philadelphia wind
where men in wigs (and silk)
endorsed a myth,
albeit one subscribed in blood
by tattered clerks and the illiterate dead.

He hugged the shilling truth of things,
sold piccolos and buns,
bought needles, ribbons, beads,
and plaster birds; lugged his cheap basket
to docks where broken Indians
or swaying rivermen brought pelts to trade
for a fictitious gleam.

In rented rooms, he beat the lurking moths
from dusty skins, piled fleece and hide
until his attic bulged like a dead zoo,
counted his flock with peasant-peering eyes,
fondled a few, sorted and groomed,
and on bare evenings warmed his sleepless
        hands
at price tags hung like windless leaves
from shapes transfigured into merchandise.

Brother Henry, too, was practical,
a sutler to redcoats at the start—

deserter when British and Hessian blood
deepened the dyer's art;

saw his fortune embellished by meat,
visited abattoir and sty,
set up shop and looked about
for cheaper sources of supply;

cantered his nag on stealthy trails,
met Tory raiders, paid in coin
for munching herds of contraband
(sweet marrow, chop, and tenderloin),

drove them through darkness
to a darker place where his shrewd knife
provided rebel and loyalist
with succulent haunches at half price,

his spraddled thumb upon the scale,
proud of his acumen and skill,
a self-made man, with a conscience as
        white
as the bones chattering after each kill.

Costume Book (Excerpt Two)

In summer, even chiefs went bare,
though seldom without the pointed jewels
of claws strung into necklaces,

or clacking halos of dead teeth
strung through their black and dancing hair.

Beaten hides of bison kept out the cold,
and their swift horns, headgear for warriors,
blazed like new moons turned into bone,
or served as flagons for an antelope's blood,
while the cosmetic bear, crowded with fat,
supplied his oozing brilliantine
to blaze on scalps and in a stone lamp's
rancid flame.
              Oar-shaped, the beaver's tail
flapped from the jerking hems of shirts,
while the eagle's hollowed wings
became a puffing painter's flute,
tube for pigments blown like colored smoke
against the borrowed skins of elk and deer
coaxed into shuffling, human shapes—
    but all forgiving, propitiated by prayer,
    their furless spirits tumbling in the palm
    of a great father overhead;
              even the fawn, weeping;
even the caribou, his sinews stretched
through a harsh needle's eye; even the parrot
plucked of his gaudy sleeves,
the puma stripped down to her steaming heart,
the ornamental porcupine—martyrs,
but reconciled, knowing the need
of naked Sioux and shivering Cherokee,

the shaman's quest of rattle, pouch, and rib,
and hearing always, above the arrow's gasp,
the ritual grunt of brute apology.

John Jacob Astor

> "John Jacob Astor, with a pack of
> Indian goods upon his back, wandered
> from the Indian trail, got lost in
> the low grounds at the foot of Seneca
> Lake in an inclement night, wandered
> amid the howl and rustling of wild
> beasts, until almost morning, when he
> was attracted by the light of an
> Indian cabin . . ."
>
> *Contemporary report*

He had no love of wilderness,
endured its weeds and waste and creaking stars
for the sake of what it held
transmutable to gold;
learned Indian dialects,
survived bad food, cold nights, and lice,
charmed squatting chiefs
with music from his flute,
a German Pan with tuftless ears,
his feet stoutly enclosed in common shoes.

Indian light amid the howl
and rustling of wild beasts,

the beaver huddled in her trap,
one foot almost gnawed free—
three paws left to dance upon
to the trills of Jacob's metal reed.

His mind moved
to its own sharp tunes,
past clubs and snares
to cosmopolitan earth:
plots and parcels of real estate—
lots in lower Manhattan
purchased "for a song"
(and currency from pelts)
in the same year
George Washington,
awkward on a New York balcony,
became the president
of town and coast and wilderness
and the bright-haired multitude of beasts
sparkling beyond the hum of mud
in savage city streets.

Triggers and shot he left to others,
mountain men brawling through thunder and spit
in pursuit of trails, prime pelts, and squaws,
and a dipper of whiskey. Their knives
were sharp as the young moon's edge,
and they left their dung in the forests
among droppings of grizzly and fox and lynx,

boasted of bears larger than mountains,
fought claw to claw with wolf and cougar,
split gut and groin without a shudder,
hollered hills down, picked their teeth with cactus,
grew great beards, swaggered like trees
in blizzards, stared into campfires
with smoke-stung eyes,
                    sometimes fearful of
                    shadows
and of certain dreams in which cubs smiled
behind the dead fortress of their mother,
and a porcupine, kerosene-drenched and lighted,
    its stiff clothes on fire
    (sport for trapper, lumberjack, and scout),
    climbed an endless pine forever
    until its bumbling torch went out.

Rich, he sailed steerage to England
to sell his harvest;
shivered below decks,
recalled an earlier voyage
(the flutes now abandoned—for a good price),
the heat of executives overhead,
swaddled himself in the memory of money made
and money to come,
    Sarah's dowry and her shrewd hands
    on fur or flesh or cabbages.

Returned. Counted his profits,

watched her fingers chuckle
among receipts and dividends.
  The million-faceted wink of gold
  shone in her eyes, gave such warmth
  even in winter, there was no need
  to squander funds on extra coal.

Played with his children,
but carried a wound
from his firstborn and namesake—
  idiot, imbecile, whatever he was,
something strange, nodding and lisping
in a private upper room.

  Invested in Greenwich Village wastes,
  and Harlem's distance-burdened hills,
  extended his realm, by land, beyond the North-
      west's river-roar
  to Canada; to the Indies and Canton, by sea,
  ships creaking with dead cargoes,
  defying embargo laws and slippery foam.

Tried to forget the noon-raw stench
of the Black Forest butcher shop,
and his grudging apprenticeship
to hanks of suet, sinews, dripping horns;
longed for prestige,
persuaded one daughter to accept
a foreign nobleman's desire,

then spent a fortune (nicked by pain)
pursuing help in health resorts and spas
for whatever moral ache Eliza found
in a royal bed;
    provided a proper funeral,
    sailed home through a hurricane shock of waves,
        offered the captain one thousand dollars,
            five thousand, ten,
                for a safe harbor—anywhere—
    was saved by the subsiding wind
    but not from the smirks of fellow passengers,
    nor from the messenger at the dock.
    Sarah's plump heart, also, was still,
        as the hearts of beavers left to rot
        where they were tossed in red and steaming
            hills.

Perceived an end to easy furs:
too many creatures killed,
too many worms with spinning mouths
replacing brilliant pelts with shining threads;
and his sea-battered colony, Astoria,
itself becoming a skeleton.
    Sold his interest, turned toward glitter of real
        estate,
    doubled and tripled his towering gold,
    commissioned a book to glorify his name,
    built his own castle, Astor House,
    foreclosed mortgages with contempt,

bought and sold
until his passionate empire rose like a great
    tomb
above the dust and drift of lesser lives.

Grew old. Grew gray. Grew thin,
though buffered by multi-million layers of fat
stored up in Wall Street vaults;
fretted about his fragile bones and breath
and his title, "Old Skinflint,"
bestowed by popular consent.
    Went bundled in glorious furs.
    Had horses, shining like machines,
    draw him through rain and sun and leaves
    (Whitman saw him once, gray gaze from under
    a broad-brimmed, beaver hat),
    fought death back as he had battled poverty,
    hired attendants (at a minimum wage)
    to toss him like a wrinkled acrobat
    on a taut blanket and so persuade
    his withered blood to circulate through wheez-
        ing veins.
        Saliva ran from a paralyzed lip as from a
            liquid spool.
        At meals, a servant, uniformed,
            guided food to the quivering mouth and gut.

In time he lived on human milk,
sucked life from the breasts

of a wet nurse.
How much the cost of this?

In time, he died,
aged eighty-six,
thin as the bones
of little animals
hollowed by the wind,
empty as a flute,
　but expensive . . .
　　thirty millions worth of dust.

Early Day Cook Book

> Yet these may ye eat of every flying
> creeping thing that goeth upon all
> four, which have legs above their
> feet, to leap withall upon the earth . . .
> *Leviticus*

. . . though not the chameleon or the mole,
weasel, tortoise, lizard and footless snail;
neither the nighthawk, the vulture, the little owl,
nor the unclean swan; but thine is the ox
(flank, the two kidneys, his fat,
the caul above the liver,
all his flesh, with his head, his legs, his marrow,
even his dung), and the flimsy goat
(rump, backbone, his beard and both his eyes)

. . . and, for some, brains of flamingos,
pâté de foi, canaries' raucous tongues—
and once, beneath the condor's swing,
the dark and booming flesh of buffalo.

> . . . the delight of an Indian gourmet
> was to eat his way down
> a ten-foot length
> of a raw, warm,
> perhaps still quivering gut . . .
>
> *DeVoto*

There were, it is said, sixty millions of them,
heads like shaggy bushes,
tails tapered to minnow size.
They, it is said, were thick as brown wind
where Boston is, Mankato, and the plains before
Denver, and past Denver to Cheyenne.
There were more of them, per square mile,
than any other living mammal. They were there
in the wind before wigwam or hogan,
herds migrating and rutting,
pawing the belly-high grass,
scraping sparks from the white glass of rivers,
stampeding and drowning in April floods,
their skeletons shaping islands
in the Mississippi and the Missouri.

Indians drove them over loud cliffs
with rattles, arrows, and plumes of fire;

they plunged, smoked, like dark meteors.

They were not diminished beyond endurance,
the ragged sunflower heads
still rearing above clubs and pits
or silver rakes of grizzlies' claws,
or the wolf's long tooth . . .

but sagged before the gray hot dust
aimed through a rifle barrel,
and perished under a racket of railroads.
The Union Pacific transcontinental
served their tongues, properly sauced, in
swaying cars.
Five hundred tongues went to England for
a royal feast,
the unspeaking carcasses left behind
to bloat like hairy thunderheads.
Teeth, horns, and hoofs made shattered cities
along the right-of-way,
while Buffalo Bill—his mustache waxed—
prepared for a wild West show,
grew fat from too much bourbon and
blood,
yet kept his pistol glittering like a star.

Even in 1871 there were dust-cloud hordes
moving their tousled foreheads and beards
into the gunshot sunrise
so that, in the following five years

two and a half million—it is all a guess—
became ghosts for nickels,
and bled for the pleasure of sportsmen
who hunted the last ten thousand down in North
    Dakota . . .
    killed one thousand the first day,
    kept trying, and, in glory,
    finished the job by mid-November
with the iced leaves rustling like breath
or the tail of a stranded minnow.

They were no longer in the wild.
    They were not anywhere
        except for a few
        hiding
        in voice-deep canyons,
        chomping on air and moonlight,
        coupling, making calves
        to be captured and reared
        between fences
        of landscaped zoos
            where popcorn drifts like snow,
            and banana peels make strange,
                slippery flowers.

                Ye may eat of every flying
                    creeping thing
                that goeth upon all four,

24

but not of the bison
for all that he has legs
to leap withal upon the measured earth.

Costume Book (Excerpt Three)

Most fun furs are fairly cheap and come
from mass-produced animals, such as the
rabbit and lamb, but on the fringes of
the fun-fur vogue are such wild creatures
as wolf, skunk, raccoon, lynx, and the
more expensive and beautiful spotted cats.

The New Yorker, May 20, 1967

The more exotic, flower-stenciled beasts,
blood still drying to garnets on their fur,
are flown direct; leopard, jaguar, and ocelot
brought on steep wings to cutting rooms
where a scent of death, like scorched hair, clings,
and yet is beaded with the armpit stench of
    swamps.

The leaf-splotched gold of eight Somali
    leopards
is needed for one coat, silent on its hanger
in the bedroom closet's motionless night,
while special hunters race to find more beasts
whose soft rosettes, made popular by Jacqueline,
are coveted by other widows, wives, and
    debutantes.

25

Of the smaller Felidae,
no larger than the moaning shapes,
that haunt our rotting alleyways
in search of fish heads shining like old tin,
twenty-five must go to make a shivering wrap
against the wind in limousines or ships.

The cheetah's silk, though it does not wear
     as well
as the leopard's flowing cloth, is "sportier"
among those who peddle such intense brocades.
Tiger skin, indelibly marked
by shafts of light and shade,
needs a special female type
to bear its wild embroidery—
     skinny, tall, with a feline slant
     around the eyes, cheekbones, or teeth.

Mountain lions, for all their grace, are difficult,
the color, like a red-brown sunset, harsh;
recommended strictly for casual dress—
ski slopes, winter golf, a northern beach,
or race tracks when the chill is deep enough.

Each year the stock goes down, the price goes up.
Broker and hunter sniff at dwindling maps,
tiptoe down trails toward things that flash like
     spotted jewels

but quake and flee, though never fast enough
to dodge the bullet's yearning arc.

The ocelot, bright black and gold,
is stacked in heaps, torn from Bolivia
and breath. The snow leopard, stretched and
    groomed,
makes a rug so deep, the appraiser's fingers
sleep in it, reluctant to wake;
so warm, it seems still wrapped around a
    heart
beating against the blue Himalayan frost.
The jaguar, mottled with pansies,
hangs from a hook beside the lynx and head-
    less wolf,
all thirst and pain removed,
insured against mildew, moths, and thieves.

Art is required to stitch invisible seams,
mend bullet scars, design the whole
to glorify a mannequin with plastic eyes
staring at lovers from her transparent cage,
the price tag delicately concealed.

The salesmen smile, inspect a credit card,
then wrap with ease, and tenderly bind
the supple prize—perfumed and plucked and
    sleek—
remote from death, it seems, of any kind.

Forms
of Travel

On the Wagon

In between drinks I go on the wagon
which is sometimes a sleigh
and always filled with children,
including me,
the ears of horses like furred leaves,
the reins black over rumps
that resemble gray, cleft apples,
the smell of leather strong as brown medicine.

It is sometimes summer
and my cousin and I
actually ride the horses
and feel their backs—
broad, alive, and separate—
under our legs
thrust out, spraddled,
like short tan oars.

Sometimes there is hay in the box,
and that is a weed-sweet, wild-smell,
hot-heady bundle
of what was rooted, clovered, seasoned,
and sickled into a great, riding pillow
where we can roll under the passing sky.

It is at other times winter
and the smoke of the horses
is like the breath of fires,
and if I could, even now,
I would sneak inside,
stow away and lean against those hearts
stroking above every kind of ice and sweat
and desire.

Cross-Country

CAUTION, the signs said.
WATCH FOR FALLING ROCK
  for livestock, horses, blood,
  and hummingbirds with jewels
    stuck to their skulls,
  a whale on the pavement (SLIPPERY WHEN
    WET),
  a salesman disguised as a poet,
  a preacher selling thorns,
  a communist with wings,
  mountain lions,
        tumbleweed,
            and witches' hats.
SHARP CURVES
  and beware of aspens dropping sparks,
  the razor-swift breath of streams,
  the sudden stumble of an avalanche—
    opals running away—
    and of a cloud's fist shaken.
FLAGMAN AHEAD
his sign a metal sun
swiveling to yellow,
blurring to gray where a hill swings a shoulder.
DRIVE SLOW: WE LOVE OUR CHILDREN

Slow across the frail jackrabbit
and the brittle skunk,
cat gut and rib sheen of mongrels,
beaks and bits of meadowlarks.
YOUR HIGHWAY TAXES AT WORK:
CONSTRUCTION FOR THE NEXT 24,830
   miles.

Pilgrimage

Seventeen miles north of Taos, on Number Three,
over gravel for the last six miles, a shrine says,
    "D.H.L."
One expects the ashes in the urn to smoke
like a whale's breath, being so torn up out of
    Eastwood earth,
unnaturally deposited on a knoll without chimneys
except the feathery stacks of trees (cedar, juniper,
    pine)
and long, cut branches with their needles arrayed
like the green spines of fish over Frieda's grave
which lies in front of the shrine-altar-sepulcher,
whatever thing it is that holds him here.

His red beard shone like the red rocks he
        looked at,
and he was, at times, a seer, and probed with
        blue eyes
deeper than those of rocks, hearing the tortoise
        cry,
named and renamed flowers, pressed them into
        words,
understood animals—a running fox himself.

A cottontail swerves down the path.

The innocent dung of a searching rodent lies
in ocher knots upon the altar ledge.
Against one wall a bird has built a clinging nest.
Under it, crossed, are two fresh boughs.
To the west the land spreads like a fallen wind-
  mill,
vanes flung toward crests purple with stillness,
and the thunderheads bunch their white brows.
Just beyond, you can dream an ocean, with bones
  and kelp at its edge;
then, still farther on, simply water, salt, and the
  sky
  rising up,
perpendicular yet arched, a blue breath over-
  riding.

The guest book had a web caught in its sleeves.
I let it be, and signed my name.

Forms of Travel

Western Pacific

moving through the dark,
the coach dark,
carrying darkness and fire wih me,
the small torch of a match struck
revealing companion shadows—
shoulders, haunches, thighs,
torsos without ears
burrowed in sleep or sorrow—
the train breathing like a horse
in a black meadow

then, outside, the ghost of a light,
knobs and knees of hills
under an ice-covered moon,
the mountains' pointed skulls invisible
but staring down and in

at my green and guilty heart.

Greyhound

home now, touched by the ocean,
I can safely remember the Christmas dust
of an interior city
and being lost in a suburb of toys

here now, rain swims down the chimney
and frogs are growing out of corners,
their beardless mouths open,
their eyes huge without spectacles

the bus took us through a sliding world,
rocks rolling like leaves in the wind,
past woman-shaped ovens made for Indian bread,
towns where TV aerials
perched in the sky like bones of new hawks
over cemeteries with crosses of sticks

here there is only the rain-crossed roof
and only a few, damp graves,
the skulls invisible but staring out.

Armchair

rocking through the firelit dark
in this leather berth,
railway tracks left to stretch
their long V's like iron geese,
the highways left to rave
across horizons piled with gifts

in this homeplace,
the house moored but moving
under the circular, wet stars,

smelling of kelp
and the rubbery breath of whales,

I watch the fire smoke
like blowing dust
and take a ship inching through the dark,
carrying darkness with me

and my red and guiltless heart.

Notice of
Change of Residence

This lion has always been with me,
grew up with me, shy, fond, or savage by turns,
a pest sometimes, a bother to the neighbors,
deep in the chest, sharp in the ribs,
at times a stench and a thunder.

He used to sleep often, tame as a haystack,
his mane dried grass to the touch,
until you brushed it once
and it flamed into this present disorder
whereby everything is rent.
Even his chains (essential now) glow
like melted branches.
My hands are raw from welding the links.
His face is as parched as an unused arrow.

This is a restricted zone
with ancient covenants.
The eviction notice is here,
and we have little time.

We need an arctic place,
unheated, apart from tinder, glance, or pulse,
cooler even than your frost-darkened eyes.

Private Beach

We had a borrowed key to the blue door
and heard the hinges roll and spit
before we reached the shore
where a sculptor had flung the waves
in running statues, or lifted driftwood up
for swinging toys.
Red tires, hung on stalks,
made rubbery planets on a post.
We rode in these as in the rings of Saturn,
drank wine, and ate a sand-blown lunch.

"Mad as a hurricane," the caretaker said.

But he was no longer there
and we were safe, walking through
crosses, guillotines, and salty slums
made out of wire, gulls' wings, cans and kelp.

His best work was the rolling shore,
orange crabs, green wind involved with surf,
the long, white rosaries of foam;
human shapes were often poor.

Journey to the Interior

You will not live here,
nor your children,
nor the old, laughing coyotes
who once sang in these hills.
We are leaving here soon,
as the grizzly left, and the condor.
(Who has seen such claws or wings?)

There is a moment yet,
before the engineers arrive,
to watch hummingbirds
strung with garnets,
madrones brown as the wrists of Indians,
bay trees that smell like green candles,
and listen again for the silence
that made a darkness for owls
with horned mouths
speaking like the E string of a guitar.

The termite with his sad drill
opposed our tenure
but could not defeat us,
nor the bats strumming their teeth
within the wall where the telephone snickers—
(they have always been there,

in strange cradles,
a tiny echo of dark wires)—
nor the wood borer on the sill
with his attic dream.

Our trunks are ready,
a funeral of hinges and locks,
stuffed with snapshots, rose pips, pencils,
and cool clothing for the desert—
the compass at hand,
the water bag hanging from the bumper
like a leaky, gray pillow.

(Who has not seen the latest clover leaf,
the wind socks, orange cheeks blown out
above the black-topped bay,
and freight trains hauling greater hills?

Who, on this coast, has heard
any word of the ocean
since the last cement truck passed,
starfish still burning in its wheels?)

For Sale:
Handyman's Special

The evening color of good-bye is deeper
when seen through scaffolding and wind,
the whipped and raging clots of leaves,
rags of blossoms, stones, a crumpled hill
(so much debris it seems we must have lugged
    it in,
carefully filed in our blind trunks),
gray nests, milkweed, a broken bottle's edge.

Bricks left over from a wing not done
lie spaced like headstones for small beasts.
Bones of a mouse—it fluttered so within the trap,
a seeming sparrow without song or beak—
resemble an abstract church
beside the sleeping cornerstone
we sweated into being and blessed
before our sight and savings failed.

From this unfinished height our eyes look down
and see our shadows hanging from the sundeck's
    rail—
and farther down, where a broken hammer leans,
the darker shadows of half-driven nails.

Sky Diver

Grotesque, jumping out
like a clothed frog, helmet and glasses,
arms and legs wading the sky,
feet flapping before the cloth flower opens;
then suspended, poised,
an exclamation point upside-down,
and going down, swaying over corn and creeks
and highways scribbled
over the bones of fish and eagles.

There is the interim between air and earth,
time to study steeples
and the underwings of birds going over,
before the unseen chasm,
the sudden jaw open and hissing.

Lying here after the last jump
I see how fanatic roots are,
how moles breathe through darkness,
how deep the earth can be.

Avalanche

The drift descends like rattling dust
from stem and bough and lofty weed,
flaps in the wind, stamps on the deck,
litters the eaves with seed and spore
and pods as dry as old canoes,
until the house creaks in the flow
sent down to us by teeming hills.

All day, all year, and in cold dreams
I fight an avalanche of lives
swarming in silk, brooding in bark,
intent on sprouting anywhere—
along the sink, beneath the door,
out of the chimney's leafless mouth,
from every wrinkle, crack, or pore,
armpit or furrow, crevice or gut,
and the grit of eyelids closed too long.

I wake up often in the dark,
alerted by a sudden field
of thistles pressed against a wall,
and smell the heat of each dry torch,
or hear beneath my silent desk
the wild cucumber's spiny purse
drag an inch forward, pause, and scrape

another step. I try for sleep
but the pillow has its nettles up,
the room is rank with sweat and thorn.

Each dawn, each day, I rise and dress,
clutch clumsy tools, use my own hands
to rake the dross from lilac beds,
spy out odd corners, scour and sweep,
uproot all vines that choke the lives
I want to keep; and yet I know
how soon, some night, the drift will flow,
pile up, and fill my seedless eyes.

Tree Service

Jockey, juggler, rider of ropes and leaves,
climber with metal thorns nailed to his feet,
he kicks dust back, stomps upward on his spurs
until his yellow bump hat bobs and gleams
among the antlers of a dying beast.

I could not save it, and it hung too near
with blackening horns aimed for the house,
but I am bothered by this hired shape
going up through the dead lace of boughs
that never felt a sharper tooth than sleet.

Yet I must back him since his life is pitched
against an overgrown and staglike head
assembling ruin above my roof,
though dreading the first severed branch
and its steep plunge.
            It falls, scattering rot
like chaff from a broken star; more sky moves in
but I miss the reaching claw. A hoof goes next—
it paced for years above my fires and mist—
and I perceive how easily space grows
around a saw.
            He swings and sears,
agile as a toy, the round hat floating

48

like a crown. I feel an office worker's awe
for his hard bustling thighs and arms.

Only the rough, round trunk remains.
A portion falls, the sound heart glowing red
against a litter of gray, scattered veins,
witness to how communication failed
between the blowing top and the dark nerves
that worked in ignorance to feed a dying crest.

The saw is still at last, and still the great stump
throbs and shines, the hidden taproot busy as
    before,
cell, core, and tissue storing useless fat.
The sky looks bare. The wind is high and keen;
it draws a knife against my back.

Heirloom

Time came in a box from out of time,
the tuneless, pulpit voice restored
that never spoke when I was green and deaf.
A gray relation wrapped it well,
a special bundle with my name. Express.
One white hair clung against its face—
his, I suppose, and soft,
but brilliant as a dying bone.

Some artisan had fixed the spring
or coil, whatever it is that makes time chirp
in a brass nest like a fanatic, garrulous snail,
and now it labors against my wall,
usurper of the living room
that once heard only rain or fire
or my breath striking its own rhymes.

The pendulum, heart-shaped, repeats
the beat and heat and nagging chime
of all those softer hearts that went
banging or ticking out of time
while this elaborate dunce stayed mute
above a clutch and swell of graves.

It clacks like some old rocking chair

or rootless teeth. (How craftily
such teeth can smile when a jaw drops.)
But I lack heart, my heart,
to burn this with the turning leaves.

It names the half hour and the hour,
timing the hummingbird and mole
(that flaming box I watch in air;
that dusty silk I cannot see,
with hands that swim through silt and nerve),
and clocks the stars, and whirrs
like breath, all breath, before it strikes.

Poetry Reading

The exact presence of poetry,
the words in the wind—
cars slanting down Van Ness,
and the walkers
like noisy shadows—
the listeners inside
hearing the man from Alaska
who smells like an iceberg.

The red jugs of wine waiting on the table.
The patience in wings,
the promise hidden in the core
of words,
and then the stumble into the dark
where we all came from.
The light-singing drive home,
the rhymed waves,
a sonnet of anchored boats,
and above us
the hung over moon
with its white
voice.

Specialists

Paul was weak on anatomy—
presumed that arteries carried air—
but felt his chest knock and perceived
that something forceful labored there

like two raw wrestlers in one room
(That which I would *not*, that I do;
that which I *would*, that I do not)
and fought to reconcile the two.

Augustine, with Bible and beard,
studied lust (his own and others),
deduced the heart was a red sty
where man and beast embraced like brothers.

Galen, grubbing, stared underneath
the flimsy coverings and saw
blood branching like a crimson tree
from head to groin, through soul and claw,

and said as much. He was not wrong,
nor Harvey when he demonstrated
the hollow pump whereby our heat
and love and ruin are syncopated.

The lub-dub beat is loud and clear;
electrocardiograms reveal
in tracings like gray lightning spines
an image of the thing we hear,
while X-rays peer through fault and rib,
expose the fatty valve and vein,
the crooked chambers, the dying will,
the whole ornate and rocking crib
that lurches us through day and dark
until the thud and murmur stop
in spite of stethoscope or pill.
Failure is certain from the start.

The ignorance of saints appalls;
one wonders how their hearts stood up
to visions on a dirty road,
or in damp cells, facing the abrupt

though buzzing knowledge of themselves;
climbed ditch and cloud, tramped on alone
toward their peculiar victories,
with one blood bank to draw upon.

Refugee

I never had the disease
but they put me there in a high bed
where my roommates played
a warped and wailing disc
(the room revolved with Peewee Hunt),
and danced their legs on a white spread
like pallid frogs—we were forbidden to walk—
and every day we had to spit for doctors
and science and for something to do
besides stare out through glass
at the same trees and the same sky
and the wind knocking its knuckles
against the motionless, brick walks.
The landscape was as pure as man could make it,
though twice a dog went down the path,
and the constant sparrows talked.

Once, there was the promise of a fire
but the engines were too swift
and we had only the thrill of wet, lean smoke.
Every Sunday there was church.
I went one time, flat on a screechy cart,
but the woman next to me, praying
before surgery, her old face ardent,
turned my heart into a fist,

and afterward I went only to the movies
(selected not to excite or depress)
and watched gunplay from my pillow,
and long, bright kisses in technicolor.

That was a castle of comfort and goodwill.
The orderlies and visitors were always cheerful.
(One nurse did the splits for our entertainment.)
The technicians smiled when they took our blood.
Even the woman who carried out the bedpans
hummed at times, blessed by no sense of smell.
At Christmas, Santa Claus, real, shook our hands
(washing his own in a basin afterward),
and the Shriners arrived in their fez hats,
encouraging us with their fat, and their pink
      smiles.

Everyone told us how brave we were
(admitting they envied our chance to rest)
and how we should inspire those with health
who yet complained or even wept
or put knives to their lusty throats,
though the chaplain said, being duty bound,
his eyes mournful behind tinted lenses,
that I had followed the wrong vision,
lived through too many midnights unredeemed
by thought of the morrow or salvation.
(Nor had I been baptized.) I was polite,

out of courtesy. He did not return,
and I was never anointed.

But I am blessed, and was,
for when priority gave me a berth
next to the window's brittle blue,
the stars were nearer. All lights went off at ten,
but not those lights,
nor the light of dawn hurrahing up
behind trees chained by nothing but their roots.
And so it was that I alone
in that November, snoring room,
watching dead boughs and my steep hall of sky,
took by surprise a keel of birds
going south in one dark, flickering V.

The sky was built of roses,
and they were angels honking on the wind.
Some things, I saw, could still be free
in spite of science, spies, or guns,
and I stood up and took my bed with me
and carried it, without a cough, outside.
I spat once only, not for laboratories
but for love, and followed those great wings
through flash and meadow, murk and sun
to where I am, and where I mean to be.

Forms
of Being

Three Predecessors

Adam

And there I was,
sitting there,
keeping to myself,
and then she came walking to me
and touched my ears and mind and mouth
and ran her hands through my hair
like a thresher, and even kissed me
before her white arms pushed me away
into the dark garden again
which was no longer filled with my own sparks
of sitting and keeping to myself,
and I went out and said to my first god,
I am yours, truly,
and was kicked by that great boot,
and so lie here
and long for her mouth
and my own mouth
kissing the dust I had before.

Noah

When the floods came
swirling like wet armor,

driving the world into the trees,
only I had a raft seaworthy;
only I knew the animals well enough—
their ways and their eyes
  and the round thoughts
in their slanted skulls;
only I could lead them out.

They smelled my own skull
rotting, and followed.
They sniffed at my heart growing,
and came leaping after,
or crawled (those lesser creatures
such as slugs and sloths),
but all arrived in time,
antelope and centipede,
and the jackal
with the laugh scarring his sad face.
I was their leader
and their eyes looked up to me,

I who every night, alone in the straw,
circled my cage
and listened for the sound of a dove
coming back, or at least going forth,
but hearing only, as now,
a dark beast snoring above.

John the Baptist

My head being separated from my body,
staring there from the platter,
it is easy enough now to see
where I made my mistake
through over-devotion to clouds or candles
and wind performing like a god
(a dust devil spinning in my brain),
to study how I might have combed my beard
      better,
used different perfumes,
or improved my haircut.
These things matter.

My eyes, still open,
are fatuous even in death
for I secretly loved the dancer
and wanted her head, soft in my hands,
and her body also in my hands
which could have preached more
than my desert-stained mouth.

I was called just and holy in my lifetime
but when the sword came down
my body rose in lust.
Observe it, daughter of water,
erect on its charger of dust.

Compound

Down here with the savages, or just the lost
  (some go naked, cling to scraps of silk, a leaf,
  a flannel suit, a policeman's badge),
Lord Jim and I; two of a kind
caught in the rattling wind and heat,
having made the wrong leap at the wrong time
in a storm-blind place.

This was a garden long ago,
but now brute monkeys swivel through the trees,
destroy all apples with their grinning teeth.
Hyenas snicker like children
whispering dirty jokes,
while the ancient overseer
(once a king; some say a god of sorts),
carrying a scepter—or is it only a Coleman
        lamp?—
patrols the littered flower beds,
inspects the rusted lock on gates
where the statue of an angel rots.

The stars are tigers' eyes.
In the center of all,
near the landing strip,
an idol shaped like a machine

sits on a greasy throne,
snores, steady as a dynamo,
while we polish one stone—
scrub, scour, invent new lies or prayers,
work at hard conscience,
polish and grind,
wash from it each midnight's mud,
hold it up, compare its gleam
to the tiger's or the idol's eye
under the dying flare
   of the overseer's light—
      Jim and you and I.

Down, Under, Above

The water world where it's deep
always has whales in it.
House wrens avoid it, and goldfish
who prefer shining where they can be seen.
It has monsters, too, seldom photographed,
and Africas of weed, kelp, rot, bones,
sea lice, hogfish, thigh-loving sharks,
and the heads of sailors.

It is too far down for most of us
lacking a talent for breath under water,
though we have been here, unescorted,
our eyes closed above our pillows.
We have seen the wink of smiles, familiar,
from the festered hold of a dead ship,
the lost nipples of torpedoes,
and armies of moss marching around us
like green soldiers. We have heard
the seashell roaring, and the lipless conch,
still inhabited, cry like a wet insect.

There have been silences, also,
and only a heart, blood-shaken,
beating deeper, darker, far down under
whale or weed,

a red knuckle drumming on a sea bed somewhere,
or tapping at a forehead—
ours or somebody's—down there, here, above,
a tiny gong in the house wren's beak
clamped shut, unsinging, high above water.

Better Homes
and Oceans

The thing was to build something there,
and keep it there, and sink the posts right,
overcome the sea, put the floor high above waves,
spray against barnacles, sharks, whales,
deter the termite, fool the thunder,
defeat the fog-glare with curtains . . .
yet keep the view.

There was so much to be
seen!

But nothing could be done about the weeds
galloping on the sea floor;
growing thicker, happy in water.

It was gold-green there, especially at morning
when the sun was right. And worth the price
(all shores are expensive) except for that seaweed
working like money, strangling vision,
bullwhip kelp dirtying the beach,
and crabs like old men hobbling through tide
    pools.

Also, at times, the house rocked like memory,
and something blind began to fuzz the ceiling.

Foundations

Houses need air underneath.
Otherwise, wood rots.
I have been alert,
knocked out the smothering blocks
false builders built.

This pickaxe has a beak
like an iron pelican.
My hands have calluses and wounds,
small price to pay
for wind beneath the floor
and a breathing roof
above all creatures there
who keep so much of the dark for us.

Interior Decoration

I am thinking of doing over my room,
of plastering wings on it,
of letting clouds in through the attic,
of collecting moles
and training them to assemble in an oval
for a rug as bright as black water:
of growing orchids under the couch
   for a lavender surprise
   against the sleeping dust;
of inviting wind to the closet—
   empty shapes will blow and sing like sails—
of planting a quail's nest in a yellow corner—
   eggs in time will hatch out stumbling flowers—
of taking a fox for a companion—
   his fur will be my fire on cold days—
of building a great square silo of books:
   pale green, blue (moss color, sky color),
   deep red, russet, orange (sun and blowing leaf
      color),
   their spines scrawled with loud gold
   and chiming silver—ARABIA DESERTA,
   LETTERS OF RILKE, WALDEN, HUNGER,
   BEYOND GOOD AND EVIL.
These, when the blizzard comes,
will be my soaring walls.

Open House

I ask the lion to come down
out of obscurity and the cold mountains,
bearing a calf or a deer
onto the sundeck
where he can sit in safety,
an almost domestic being
with blood on his paws
and his whiskers shining
like the fine hairs on rope.

For this I might sacrifice
the chicken in the freezer,
or the lunch reserved
for our spoiled kittens
who yearn to be lions
but cannot conquer
their lust for cans
packed with tuna
and the long, green bones of mermaids.

Deities

One wrinkled god
stands beside the scorpion's tail,
half holds it up, instructs the uncertain head
which way to turn
toward what is dark or wet.
Another holds the trout's jaws wide
until the hook arrives.

Some ride with camels
(spit from sandy throats),
warble in nests with mice,
wake with the junco,
put fists in cyclones,
peel the long bark from birches,
push at grass,
pry open the sluggish iris,
teach rain to tap-dance
and the lightning how to leap
like nerves in a furnace.

One, stunted, climbs
the neck of the giraffe.
One, squinting, has made the cat
and us
see more of night than we require.

Dreamers

My dreams are guilty,
dangerous,
peculiar shapes
hanging on walls,
long hair whipped into gray flags,
anxiety, ache, and scheme,
a nail in the ankle,
eyes seen in dirty mirrors.

Dawn reprieves
with common sun
   and the talk of quail
   making a fussy, brown lace.

These lend grace.

Even at midnight,
   the owl defends—
   feathered counsel
   with a judge's beak—
himself a gobbler of innocents,
   swaying
in his own dangerous dream.

Is Is Like Is

Voices of birds are
voices of birds,
and leaves speak always like leaves,
and water is forever water
though it may hold me and my eyes
and let wind shape it.
The birds are now,
not tomorrow or yesterday,
not in anybody's grave singing,
but here where the sun is only sun
with all the trees making tree shadows
under the swinging shadow of one cloud,
and blue chairs on the deck
quietly being blue chairs,
though holding the forms
of people who have sat there
listening to bird voices and leaf talk
and holding in turn the sunlight
surrounding the dark room
where hearts beat
like all hearts,
like birds, leaves, and water.

Sequoia Gigantea

They keep to themselves, these giants,
obsessed with growth; great stalks and stilts,
taller than silos, rounder,
sinewed, gristled, hide thicker than a whale's,
groaning upward five thousand years,
flecked and plated and ribbed,
trunks flared like a rose-brown elephant's foot
to support a leafy, light-blown crown.

I stood under one. Against my hand
I felt the surge of veins, long freight trains
lumbering toward the top, lugging blind food
through vascular bundles, cortex, cells,
to that branched head nodding above its monstrous
     neck.

Some embryo creaking when Christ was born
had gone awry. Some wish had overreached its
     mark.

Alchemist's Notebook, Revised

You shall take sleek bolts of metal
named after the seven planets or classical gods
or perhaps a great business,
and place them in silos of earth
from whence they may be delivered
by the tempest of a finger
unto the non-believing nations.

This is a newly sacred art
and though there are many disciples
the chosen are mechanics with large thumbs.
Only the initiates, blue-eyed, athletic,
familiar with uniforms and the skins of metal,
know the secret of the right lever.
Two to a crucible, they shall consult
the eyes and forehead of the other
before they release the world from its hinge
whereby we shall be defended against the
     aggressor
and brought into another dimension
even as the birds, our nimble brothers,
and the awkward, though lately risen, ape.

Continents shall be broken like paper islands.

Blood will replace the fire in rivers.
A mist shall rise over the dried oceans
in the shape of the *materia prima*
which the old alchemists,
consorting naïvely with souls and tinctures,
presumed they could find in gold,
lead, salt, vinegar, pus, sky,
or the rotted teeth of an aged, blind lion.

Everywhere now you must plant death
like wheat grain in the very dark earth
which Adam took with him to Paradise—
nigrum nigruis nigro—black blacker than black.

Lead, the salt of all metals,
contained, they said, a radiant white dove.
Quicksilver, if quick enough, could be changed
into the savory flesh of God.
Crumbs of communion. Plasma of bread.
Steel, we know, is seed and savior,
disciplined, rain-proof, alert, containing
sperm of fire to fructify the world.
And gold, if studied closely,
conceals enough of Christ,
the *anima aurea* which all seek for,
caught in a coin no larger than His eye.

This is alchemy. This is power.
When rainwater stinks after ten days,

cooped in non-returnable bottles,
pour it out under a waning moon.
When Titan snores in his upright cradle,
press a button lest your dreams awake you.

The unicorn permits no other in his cave,
as the Son of God permitted no other in the
    womb
He inhabited. Earth and Virgin are the same,
though earth now has many sockets, a metal
    son in each.

Each shall rise, tall Titan and his progeny,
Minuteman and Thor.
              Hallowed shall be the
  fire
if we shoot first and win.

This earth was built on the ruins of another,
and voices are buried under the living rocks.
"Who is near unto me is near unto the Fire,
And who is far from me is far from the
  Kingdom."

Wheels revolve through Nevada dust.
The orbit and cross are drawn.
Iron snails of bulldozers crawl
over Indian bones, preparing graves
for our soon-to-be risen souls.
Ghosts of rain dancers and alchemists leap

like smoke from a special, fermenting cup.
    Such rain must stink.
    "When this has happened,
    let a drop of consecrated wine
    into the wet; then thou wilt see at once a mist
    and a heavy darkness above on the water
    such as there was also in the first creation."

The steel iris bulbs, hidden,
wait for their season to sprout.
We shall be united some hour with the heavens.
Through hail we may see the red rain fall
thickened by withered and withering sparrows,
families, friends, and realms of paper
melted into a robe of white thunder.

Titan, our root, we are at thy service.
Minuteman, make certain of the hour.
Earth, our Adam, we must thee transfigure
into thighbones and blood, mist and knuckles
of children dead but with mouths as wide open
as those of frogs, or as that of the green-haired
king of the unconscious sea
who sat and still sits
with his jaws agape
to devour his weed-robed, returning son.

    A heavy night shall hang above the water
    such as there must be in the last creation.

Subdivider

I smell the dust of stones in sunlight,
and the dust under them,
and the dust under my eyes
and running in my palms,
and crickets buried deep under tar,
the dust of their tiny hoofs,
and the ashes of orchards.

This desert is new.
Some bones are still pink;
little eyes drift in the wind
of our many machines.
At times I have seen an embroidery of nerves
scrawled in the rocks,
or garlands of fur drying
on a lattice of ribs.
So many have died recently;
so many are still dying.

The bulldozers work ten hours a day
though the hearts of birds are very small.
My hand against my face, even at dawn,
smells like a grave.

I, Alexander Hamilton, Under This Stone

This darkness, though closer, is not unlike
certain black nights on the Christiansted wharves,
slaves arriving, invisible except for eyes
that shone white as almond-shaped fish;
nor is the dust tang here stronger
than the silks and sweat hanging
in the closets of planters' wives,
only deeper, colder, packed down, never moving
as those gowns and hot cargoes moved;
   more earth now than dust, more death than
      darkness,
   more rot than bone, eyelid, or liver,
   and my voice no louder than a mole's.

   Absurd that the dead should speak at all,
      or try, jaws creaking like the hinges
   of an old jewel box; absurd that one should
      die
   from choice, and worse to wonder
   whether it was either noble or wise.
                  I should have demurred,
   though lots were cast, at having to face
   a rooster-loud sun, and waves brighter

than a field of blue swords. Trees gave my
        enemy
a summer's shield. I stood exposed
like a weed in winter, mirrored by rock,
poised on those Heights where my bronze
        bust leans
above the roar of worm and tunnel—
was broken there, reared upward on my toes
at the lift of the bullet, sent my own shot
into branches. A bird woke, spinning,
above Burr's head and spoke to the wind—
or the wind spoke to it—as the false world
        splintered
and I fell forever.
                        Air tasted like blood.
The wound was mortal, as was the first
        wound
when I said, "Father," and no one answered,
nor ever did, though I hunted for him
through Colony and Kingdom, wrote words
        into mist,
aspired and invented, hauled a ghost with me
even to Weehawken. There he died, yet
        through me lived
if his name was the same as mine.

Hamilton—aide-de-camp, statesman,
lawyer, lover; how often I wrote it
but perhaps should have written

Walsterstorrf, Stevens, perhaps *Levine*
or ALEXANDER SONOFAWHORE.

This darkness I was born in.
If and when all dust is risen,
to whose strange arms shall I ascend?

California,
Here I Am

The boat comes home full of blood,
the hero (Hamilton) still alive in his silk
and his powdered hair,
the Hudson not as blue as before.
                    That was in summer.

Here in this fall, by this pool,
far from New Jersey and falling leaves,
farther still from Valley Forge
and those huts without windows,
and almost beyond recall of any revolution,
how silly it seems:
not only him and his duel, but us,
the hog call of cars,
the banks of blood darkening,
the tracks on the vinyl floor,
the wall to wall tombs,
even the hours by the television set
where real deaths happen
at high noon and midnight.
(He did die, of course. It was long ago.)

The pool is a lifesaver,

shaped like a kidney, almost clean of leaves.
I plunge. The Pacific splashes,
blue as it was before.

State Hospital
Therapeutic Community Council

The demented council meets on folding chairs
each Tuesday afternoon at three,
led by the paranoid president,
survivor of shock therapy
(electric punishment for sins,
the voltage measured by engineers;
a crooning noise, but growing shrill
when its hot tooth dips down and sears).

Only professionals would guess that he
(such normal eyes and mouth and hair)
had ever played with knives, or rocked
like a blind doll some pet despair,
although there is a certain look—
touched by wires, a splinter's gleam—
behind his smile.
                      Yet what of the nurse,
her strange deep stare? And what of the scream?
It came or seemed to come
from the staff psychiatrist
bent over his notes, sweat in his beard,
and a white scar glowing on his wrist.

All are in danger here,
but only some can name their fears
for a brooding secretary to record.
Common pencils may be spears
with acid tips. Postage stamps
must be used with care. The arsenic is there,
supplied by Jews or the Red Guard,
and deadly fallout is everywhere.
The dark vice-president, her inky hair
protected by a metal hat, watches for spies
and saboteurs, facing the constant enemy—
the look and gleam and thrust of human eyes.

Only we outside, safe from shock,
being oriented toward reality,
can see things as they are—the blood,
the searching flames, the noose in every tree.

Note to the Outside

Long before anyone knew I was mad
I used to talk to beetles
and trees or whatever would listen.
I never did address God, however,
who has stone ears
and, in any case, is not concerned.
I had many strange loves
and pursued them like a hunter,
did well by them,
and went back to my work the better for it.

That was before.

One love failed
and in going over the failure,
over and over in my deepening mind,
with the rain beating
and the branches of trees falling,
and the beetles weeping like small girls
in bronze dresses,
I discovered what I had always known,
that nothing and no one had truly listened,
and that no one had trembled
as I did—and do—at the fox sparrow's breast
when he comes to this cage,

or the sun rising like an orange city
over any field anywhere.
Even in darkness I see it;
it is rising and singing, for me.

Justice

It is, of course, a human question
the wolf does not solve,
nor the rabbit digesting flags of clover.
The grave is certain
for talent or wisdom
or the zest of the trout
who seeks in the hook
a shining equation of his hunger.

The rustle of mouths,
whether of judge or attorney,
rapist or lover,
or simply the mistaken
who aimed a gun
they thought was unloaded,
wait upon other mouths—
smack of the jawed dust
that opens and closes,
suck of rain,
chatter of mice in a crowded attic,
and the unsinging idiot
that walks on his belly,
unmoved by wigs or habeas corpus.

Praise, then, the maggot

in his dirty clothing,
for the lisp is forgotten
in the roar of harvest,
and judgment waits on his low sickle.

Hunter's Cabin

The deer horns on my fence,
sharp as the skeleton of a hand,
turn green in winter rain,
part moss, part bone,
part something else not fastened there
but running fast through loam and spit
and sparks of blood.

I half expect such things to sprout,
become a stem or leaf,
or suddenly a savage head,
the nostrils warm and steep,
ears strung with hair,
the brown teeth arched.

Wind plucks the chicken wire
like a hoof,
and the horns clack.
A forehead gleams and grows
in my black woods.
The large, dead eyes look out.

Snob

The snail that I took from a black corner
(if it was a snail) seemed a round coffin.
In the sun a wet flower oozed out
and there were five small horns
the color of pewter,
but nothing recognizable as a forehead
or heart. Whatever it was, fleshlike,
it quivered and shone, filled with muddy
    diamonds,
then felt my shadow—or some other—and slid
    back
into itself, never speaking
nor making one gesture to show that it saw me
or heard. I was snubbed.
               Lie there, cousin,
in your swirled and brittle grave,
tongueless, loving only darkness and wet
and whatever you imagine you were born to say.

Grade AA, Large

A chicken glows in the knuckle of this egg.
I hold it to the light
and see a map of feathers, blood, and beak.
Shall I eat it
and raise a rooster under my heart
to cry, every morning,
like a new nail in my throat?

Séance

Something, somebody, is trying to speak through
    me—
ant or ape or a great-grandmother,
perhaps a voice even older,
perhaps the sea, perhaps a throat in the sea,
perhaps a shape without eyes or thumbs,
dust, maybe, or some ancient crab
hobbling sidewise on his skinless knuckles.

When I try to speak for myself
there is a crackle and a hum.
Bones appear in my voice and break
and another voice rattles.

I have wakened at night
and heard weeds chanting on my pillow
or birdlike things with notes as bright as new
    straw,
and a creature very wrinkled and huge
groaning like a mountain with a wound in its side.

Double Vision

Sitting looking at myself
I perceive flesh,
and bone behind the flesh,
and then nerves, gristle, ganglia,
and finally a second creature
looking at me through my own eyes.
  This could be a cricket
  with multiple-faceted vision;
  this could be a toad
  half-blinded by a dream of flies;
  this could be a mastadon
  snoring with decay;
  this could be a fun house pool
  deep as a mirror.

  This could be, simply,
  the sad and cross-eyed gaze
  of a baboon scratching its belly,
  poised in a false tree,
  before it swings downward
  to stare across an island moat
  toward watchers on the other side.

Childhood Scenes

Snapshot

There I stood, wet ruffles to my knees,
my skirt tucked up above the lake
where the black-burned ghosts of trees
made an upside-down forest,
my toes among the branches,
and minnows bumping my flesh sometimes,
soft as eyelashes—at most a prickle
like that of a child's sparkler
shedding its delicate stars.

That lake is all lakes forever,
though others have been colder, deeper.
Since then I have plunged over my head,
to cellars of weed, touched by windless rot,
grazed fish larger than my grown body,
felt the draft of their slamming gills,
and surfaced, breathless, wearing the water's look
in my eyes.
        The snapshot holds me still,
and what I saw there, looking down through
    inches
as green as the thinnest slices of cucumber
one on top of another, the scent of shallow waves

like mowed grass, the sound that of wet leaves
slapping in rain—and mother or grandmother or
    uncle
pointing a black box—and no thought then
of another box with its long shutter closing.

Flight

The time my grandfather strapped
a clumsy hive of chickens to the car,
bulging and loud and live behind the trunk,
the nucleus for another start
toward country treadmills sprouting gold
(where we had squatter relatives),
I thought those stubby wings might help us rise
above the ruts that former lives had made.

They neither flew nor sang.
He might as well have packed a crate of dust
except for chucks and sighs and the raw yell
the cock kept up. The hens were speckled rocks
and if they moved they hunted lice beneath their
    sleeves,
or pecked a fainting sister's head.
They were not pets, nor were they wild,
but prisoners (once swift on Asian slopes)
descended to a siloed land, half bird, half slave
to grain and sea-gray oyster shells.
Their eyes were all that kept a windy gleam.

We rode on tires dutifully in touch
with gumbo, rock, and sand, a cargo driven into
    pines,
crude dreams of wealth and corn
and loon-escorted skies.

We all had cousins where we disembarked.
Theirs were feathered. Mine were snub-kneed,
hostile, bare. Each had to fight
for what he grubbed from that mean air,
chicken or child.
           The snow fell soon,
as blue as beaks or an angel's eyes,
and shovels scraped a path toward heavy barns.
In the safe coop, hens worked like boats
and laid their eggs as they were bound to do
while the cock dreamed on a low stump.

I raced alone to one unbroken drift,
unseen, unknown, and lay face up.
My spine a fern against the fallen cold
I danced cloth arms on that white cloud, and flew.

Listener

The cottonwoods always clanged,
their tin leaves beating the clouds.
Below, their roots like a giant's veins
lifted the sidewalks,

and farther down pried wells apart
and creaked through the brown bones
of Indian patriots who died
before the flags and silos came.

All night, some nights, above my bed
the branches of one tree complained,
grew hoarse with talk,
gossiped with wind,
lost leaves as yellow as old teeth,
clattered like a cart,
clicked—sometimes sighed—and kept my world
      awake.
  How much quieter the lilac leaves were
  with their green bat's ears cocked,
  the patient creak of cabbages
  in the garden alongside,
  and the sputter of carrots
  like orange soldering irons
  plunged into water.

My heart beat like a rock
enclosed in felt, less deep than graves
or wells, but with its own noise pitched
against a garrulous night
that listened only to itself.

Who Loves to Lie with Me

Studying the ground,
my forehead almost on it,
my lips near needles, moss, rock-rust, litter,
I am amazed at how much there is to it,
how much lost and left
and yet building up into turrets,
mosques, patios, even rainbows
where the lashed light touches
the smallest of weed flowers.
The base of the wild iris
is nearly the color of my blood,
but at the top
it is pale seawater,
color of green thought,
almost a tip of consciousness;
and life bumbling
beneath my eyebrows,
bee and slug, flea and cricket,
the lugging ants, the drunken-legged spiders,
and there in a dust corner
the cast-off husk of some small star
like a brown beetle.

There is such a buzz here;
my ears whirl with it,

and the wind spinning it
into legs, arms, squeaking trees,
motes, mites, and the precise blue tick
inside my wrist, my temple—
the same inside you
with your forehead and mouth beside me
and your eyes watching me
watch the rounded earth
where the lizards run,
their tongues flicking what seems sunlight
and is love.